1976

Thimble Treasury

Myrtle Lundquist

Copyright © 1975
Myrtle Lundquist

Library of Congress Number
75-21332
ISBN: 0-87069-123-6

Photography by
Duree Studio
Ottumwa, Iowa

Author "The Book of a Thousand
        Thimbles" 1970

Published by

Wallace-Homestead

Wallace-Homestead Book Company
580 Water's Edge Road
Lombard, IL 60148
Printed in U.S.A.

ACKNOWLEDGMENTS

Gratitude is expressed to the thimble groups, museums, experts, and collectors for their cooperation in supplying data used in this book. Indebtedness is acknowledged to all who graciously afforded access to their collections and scrapbooks.

Mrs. Roz Belford
Mrs. Grace Cottrell
Mrs. Lorraine M. Crosby
Mrs. Thomas J. Cullen
Mrs. Ida Dornbos
Mr. Walter L. Eppel
Mrs. Kenneth Erdmann
Mrs. Evelyn Eubanks
Mr. Conan E. Fisher
Mrs. Lucille Fisher
Ms. Ursula Hildt
Mrs. Emily B. Hunt
Mrs. Leasa E. Jennish
Mrs. Anna E. Johnson
Mrs. Ruth Marr

Mrs. Chiyoko Oda
Mrs. Joann Ryan
Mrs. Elizabeth G. Sickels
Mrs. Donald H. Scott
Ms. Helen Taylor
Mrs. Charles W. Thompson
Mrs. Nina Tillman Vaughn
Mrs. Faye Walton
Mrs. William B. Weiss
Mrs. Bonnie Whildin
Mrs. Frieda Whitaker
Mr. Fred N. Whiting
Mrs. Lucile P. Whiting
Mrs. Gladys Zabriskie

British Museum, London
Christie, Manson & Woods, Ltd., London
T. J. Cullen, Jeweler, Winnetka, Illinois
Duree Studio, Ottumwa, Iowa
Field Museum of Natural History, Chicago
Hugo Morley-Fletcher, London
The Hyde Collection, Glens Falls, New York
Munson-Williams-Proctor Institute, Utica, New York
Museum of Fine Arts, Boston
Prudential Insurance Co., Newark, New Jersey
Renssalaer County Historical Society, Troy, New York
Science Museum, London
Simons Bros., Philadelphia
Victoria and Albert Museum, London
Washington Historical Society, Washington, Connecticut

T	Thimbles arouse memories of a person, place or thing.
H	History obscures the contributions of small necessities to the progress of civilization.
I	Intrinsic value of thimbles is often subordinate to the study of people who owned them.
M	Meditating on the story of a thimble may revise a sense of values.
B	Beauty and excellence are reflected in the practical characteristics of thimbles.
L	Lifestyles of ancient eras included use of thimbles.
E	Education of children frequently began with use of a thimble to work the alphabet on a sampler.
S	Sentiment is inherent in thimbles.

CONTENTS

COVER PICTURE: Top center, read clockwise: (1) Lace edge, Celtic crosses, Gabler; (2) Enamel, Norway; (3) Enamel with palms; (4) Damascene; (5) Parthenon; (6) Brass, star knurling; (7) Dutch scene; (8) Altantic Cable Thimble. Inside circle, top: (1) Gold with diamond settings; (2) Covered bridge; (3) Stitch-in-time thimble; (4) Gold, Israel.

INTRODUCTION

THIMBLE TREASURY is for the experienced collector, new collectors, and non-collecting spectators who have a zest for searching along the roads of history.

The purpose of this book is to present photographs and data derived from many sources. Information pertaining to some aspects of thimble collecting is not readily available.

The focus is on thimbles in a perspective that embraces a wide range of subject matter. Facts are pursued in several areas of art, craftsmanship, and social relations. Few items can claim the varied facets found in thimbles. Rare thimbles are pictured as well as thimbles included in many collections.

The experienced collector constantly enhances his knowledge with pictures of rare items or examples sought.

New collectors are introduced to categories and avenues of approach.

Non-collectors may find nostalgic interest in associations and sentiment.

A thimble stimulates curiosity about fields of endeavor and social strata in history. There is scarcely another collector's item so ancient in history, so sentimental in aspect, or so universal in utility.

THE BOOK OF A THOUSAND THIMBLES published in 1970 by Wallace-Homestead Book Company, Des Moines, Iowa, presents one personal collection and some well-known thimbles in museums.

THIMBLE TREASURY presents herein additional items and data from a number of exceptional personal collections as well as from collections in museums. Many are rare thimbles or have some special significance. Descriptions or identifications are by the collectors who contributed data.

CHALLENGES

The thimble collector frequently asks, "What is it made of?" "Where and when was it made?" and "Who made it?"

In the style of a journalist covering the W's in a story, there follow descriptions, purposes, chronology, geographical locations, and makers.

What is it?

A thimble may be defined as a sewing tool. The name is found in many languages. In German "fingerhut," literally "finger hat," is descriptive. In Japanese "yubi-nuki" means "finger-put-through." Byswaim (finger-guard) and gwinadur (sewing steel) were early words in the English language. Samuel Pepys mentioned thimbles in his diary of 1663.

Thimbles evolved through the ages from bone to bronze to precious metals, and from simple to ornate design.

To mend sails, a thimble called "sailor's palm," usually made of leather or brass, was used. A modern version may be purchased today in some sporting goods stores. Large thimbles of bronze were used by rugmakers and tapestry workers.

Why was it made?

The collector in his zeal sometimes overlooks the reason for the thimble's existence. It was needed by the people who used it.

The universal need for thimbles to protect fingers and facilitate sewing has existed since human beings began to sew pelts together for warmth and survival. Thimbles of pre-recorded history were probably stone or bone.

Much later, the desire to make surroundings pleasant motivated decorative stitchery at isolated places on the globe.

Constant pushing of the needle necessitated protection of fingers.

Where or when was it made?

One of the oldest thimbles extant is an Egyptian stone thimble now in the Metropolitan Museum of Art.

Bronze thimbles buried by the eruption of Mount Vesuvius in 79 A.D. were exhumed during excavations at Herculaneum and Pompeii.

Two large cast bronze thimbles, circa thirteenth century, now in the Victoria and Albert Museum, London, may have been used by tentmakers of nomadic people near Cordoba, Hispano-Moresque.

Thimbles existed in the Orient and Europe before there was communication between the continents.

Marco Polo brought exquisite embroidered silks from his travels in China, and soon sailing vessels began the trade that was to stimulate production in many fields. Samples of embroidery were exchanged. Surely some sort of thimble was used to make the elegant samples of needlework carried both ways by sailing ships.

Who made it?

One can only conjecture about makers of unmarked thimbles. Identity may sometimes be determined by the location in which it is found, as in the case of Indian relics.

If an item has been in a museum for a length of time, the style or material might match a new-found specimen which has been identified.

Where to start?

It is advisable to keep a record of items in a collection. This may start as a simple notebook or card index.

In numerical order, columnar fashion, list the date acquired, from whom, a short description, and, if purchased, the price. Some records contain meticulously drawn sketches.

Receipts are documentary evidence and may be of value in obtaining insurance.

A card index is convenient for some purposes such as a cross reference or categorizing.

As a collection grows, identifying numbers should be placed in or on the item.

The manner of keeping a record is a personal preference.

SEARCH AND RESEARCH

The study of thimbles relates lifestyles and ideals of the past to contemporary environs. Thimbles play an important role in the saga of civilization.

The flow of curiosity meanders in a fashion which sooner or later begins to follow a definite direction, influenced perhaps by individual discrimination or experience.

Thimble collecting is a fairly new field open to people of every age and educational, social, or economic level. Manners of approach are individual. With some researchers, it is sufficient to enjoy and admire items in museums or in collections. Possession is not the essence of appreciation.

Searching for items is adventure. As with many achievements, the place to start is usually at home. From home, the leads abound to antique shows, dealers, flea markets, clubs, contacts through correspondence and advertising.

Acquiring items is one of the constructive satisfactions of exploration.

The lure of the quest often results in warm friendships. A common interest is a bond.

Some collectors seek art forms and eventually gravitate to a particular category. Occasionally a unique item becomes the nucleus of a special category.

Seeking, studying, comparing and categorizing items, much as a scientist uses inquiry, provides satisfaction.

Collectors are scientists in a way. Collecting any item is accompanied by gathering of data. Similarities and differences are noted. All collectors seem to become selective.

There is no one so miserly as a thimble collector with a rare or hard-to-find thimble.

No one feels more generous than a thimble collector who will part with ten or fifteen give-away thimbles to help a young new collector get started.

Let is be said that it is important to weigh phases of collecting against one's lifestyle in a realistic manner. A whole new world of attitudes, values, and satisfactions have been known to emerge through the pursuit of thimble collecting.

EXAMPLES OF THIMBLES AND ACCESSORIES

One of the fascinations of collecting thimbles is the variety of examples. Many social strata are represented in a stream of history going back to pre-recorded times.

The variety of examples represented in collections should afford pleasure to the experienced as well as to the beginning collector.

Some rare items may be one-of-a-kind extant.

More plentiful objects afford material for the new collector.

Commemorative thimbles usually represent a special event. Collectors interested in history are particularly attracted to these.

Souvenir thimbles are mementoes of places, a monument, or attraction of interest which may have changed over many years and is not easily identifiable.

Porcelain thimbles of the 1700s with miniature paintings of occupations may afford information in the field of sociology.

A plain or worn utilitarian thimble may have belonged at one time to a famous person.

Related artifacts include the thimble-shaped aperture in a sewing box or workbasket, the thimble long gone. At The Hermitage in Tennessee, home of Andrew Jackson, seventh president of the United States, there is a sewing pouch in every bedroom and a magnificent sewing box in the ladies' parlor, but there are no thimbles. Much beautiful sewing is evidenced by quilts and coverlets.

The "Stitch-in-Time" thimble, coveted by collectors, is inscribed with lettering which resembles the framed embroidered turn-of-the-century mottos which decorated many a "Home Sweet Home."

The Dorcas thimble is a favorite collectors' item. Many churches have a Dorcas Sewing Circle, named for the disciple named Tabitha, which by translation is called Dorcas (mentioned in The Bible, Acts 9:36-38). Dorcas was the woman who devoted

11

herself to good works and acts of charity. The Dorcas thimble was made by Charles Horner, Chester, England, in three layers, the middle one steel for hard wear. It was patented in England June 14, 1884.

The Liberty Bell thimble, inscribed "Proclaim liberty throughout all the land unto all the inhabitants thereof" (Leviticus 25:10), has been reproduced and is a popular collectors' item.

Shown in following pages are examples of thimbles which collectors dream about. A number of photographs represent individual thimbles assembled from various collections. Some photographs with no credit line are from private collections. Identifications are by the donors.

Thimble Holders

A wide variety of thimble holders may be traced from the Victorian era. Original cases with matching thimbles frequently indicate the maker's mark only on the case. This has been one source of dating for matching unmarked thimbles.

Jewel-studded custom made thimbles were presented in a distinctive case, not always matching, not always of the same metal, but elegant.

Decoration often relates to a period of popular fashion.

Slippers of various designs and materials were in vogue for many uses during the 1890s. Early glass slipper keepsakes suggested the Cinderella Story.

Acorn and walnut designs were plentiful in the nineteenth century, as were the egg-shaped, purse type and leather brass bound cases. Egg-shaped holders may have been modeled from the ornate Russian Easter egg.

Silver cases from England, bog oak from Ireland, Mauchline ware from Scotland, porcelain from France and Germany are treasured by collectors.

SLIPPER THIMBLE HOLDERS

THIMBLE HOLDERS AND ETUI

13

THIMBLE HOLDERS ON OPPOSITE PAGE

TOP ROW: (1) China blue boy, Germany. (2) Carved wood. (3) Real walnut shell with drawstring pouch inside. (4) Blue glass, modern.

SECOND ROW: (1) Sweetgrass basket. (2) German silver sewing kit with thread on winders and tiny spools. (3) Blackthorn.

THIRD ROW: (1) Red plush. (2) Vegetable ivory. (3) Blue plush.

FOURTH ROW: (1) Marbleized German sewing kit. (2) Carved ivory acorn case. (3) Pink sewing kit, Japanese.

FIFTH ROW: (1) Hand carved wooden case. (2) Yellow enamel sewing case with scissors. (3) Crown stand, modern.

SIXTH ROW: (1) Child's thimble in original box, size 3. (2) Red leather case, purple velvet lining. (3) Gold egg-shaped holder with rhinestone trim. (4) Black leather case, purple velvet lining. (5) Slipper holder of printed silk.

BUCKSKIN DRESS decorated with thimbles acquired by the Field Museum of Natural History, Chicago, November 1900. The costume was believed to be 100 years old when acquired.

All are 14K and 18K gold.

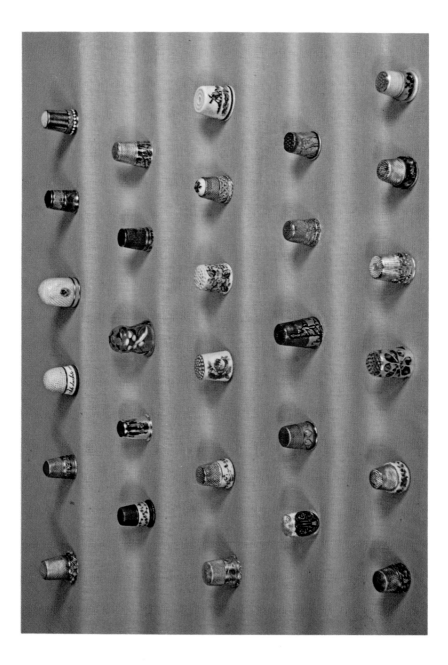

TOP ROW: (1) Germany "modern" sterling, gold band with raised blue settings and blue stone top. (2) Old sterling, six-pointed stars, shield, carnelian top. (3) Old Meissen, crossed swords, appears to be stoneware, inscription in German.. (4) Mother of Pearl, pansy medallion, two gold bands, circa 1790. (5) Sterling, wide band, hammered rim, carnelian top. (6) Enamel blue stone top.

SECOND ROW: (1) Gabler Bros. sterling, enamel band, rose garland. (2) Germany, modern, monogrammed, red stone top. (3) Blown glass, modern, four colors. (4) Old England, Goldstone top. (5) Gabler Bros., baby head.

THIRD ROW: (1) DAR thimble, Constitution Hall, Memorial Centennial Hall. (2) Brass, modern, enamel band, rose and forget-me-not. (3) Porcelain bisque, modern, hand-painted, dated 1972. (4) Porcelain bisque, hand-painted, forget-me-not, 1970. (5) Brass, modern, Switzerland, stars on band, ornate rim, petit-point. (6) Porcelain, modern, Delft blue windmill farm scene, Holland.

FOURTH ROW: (1) Embroidery Guild thimble. (2) Brass, hearts on band. (3) Bicentennial Statue of Liberty, gold clad Continental silver, by a French silversmith. New York skyline around band. (4) Gold, scenic. (5) Old sterling, Denmark, overlapping plume-leaf design on side, jade top.

FIFTH ROW: (1) Sterling, raised grape. (2) Brass, modern, petit-point. (3) Mexican, modern, abalone insets. (4) Shrine of Our Lady of Fatima, Portugal. (5) Brass, modern, petit-point. (6) Sterling, modern, Delft blue windmill scene, blue stone top, marked Germany.

19

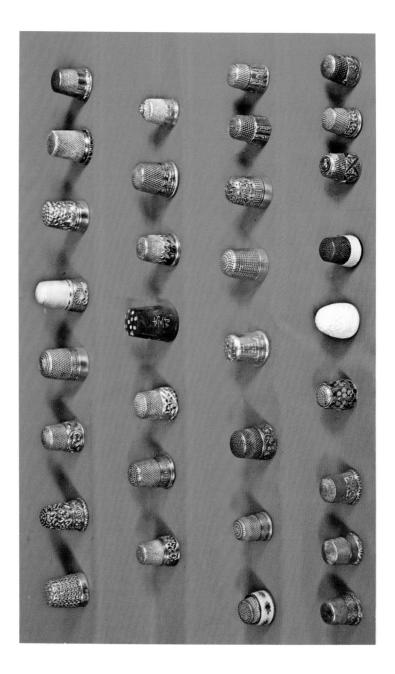

TOP ROW: (1) Sterling applied discs of silver, hand indented, England. (2) Tall, sterling, ornate sides and top, floral band. (3) Sterling, wide gold band, rococo. (4) Sterling, inscribed "James Walker, the London Jeweller." (5) Tall, sterling, shell on wide gold band, gold lined. (6) Heavy sterling, floral circles below large diamond-shaped knurling, plain rim, England. (7) Gabler Bros., sterling, gold lined, one row marcasite. (8) Gold-plated. Waite-Thresher.

SECOND ROW: (1) Gabler Bros., gold-lined, applied floral band, inscribed "Good Luck" with horse-shoes. (3) Sterling, Ketcham-McDougall, wide Rococo band, Louis XVI rim. (4) Large jade, with Chinese characters. (5) Sterling, Simons Bros., fleur-de-lis pattern which extends up into knurling. (6) Gold leaf and berry band. (7) Sterling Liberty Bell thimble inscribed "Proclaim Liberty in the land to all the inhabitants. By order of the Assembly of Pennsy. in Phila. 1752."

THIRD ROW: (1) Sterling, collapsible thimble, enamel floral band. (2) Brass, "Fare Well" with forget-me-nots on band. (3) Sterling, plume-type gold band, "Clara." (4) Pyramid of native stones at equatorial Ecuador. (5) Sterling, plain waffle-type knurling. Abel Morrell, "Doris." (6) Sterling, all-over floral circles above waffle band, plain rim, Abel Morrell, "Doris." (7) Simons Bros., Sterling with wide gold panelled band, "Pat. May 28, 1889." (8) Sterling, Scenic Towers, dated Sept. 20, '81.

FOURTH ROW: (1) Sterling, Waite-Thresher, geometric wheel design. (2) Gold, Simons Bros., plain band, Ornate rim. (3) Sterling, anchor band. (4) Russian or Greek enamel. (5) Carved walrus tusk. (6) Sterling. Plain pink enamel band. (7) Simons Bros., sterling, wide gold band. (8) Gold-filled, leaf design. (9) Sterling, wide gold band, scroll "J.C.P."

21

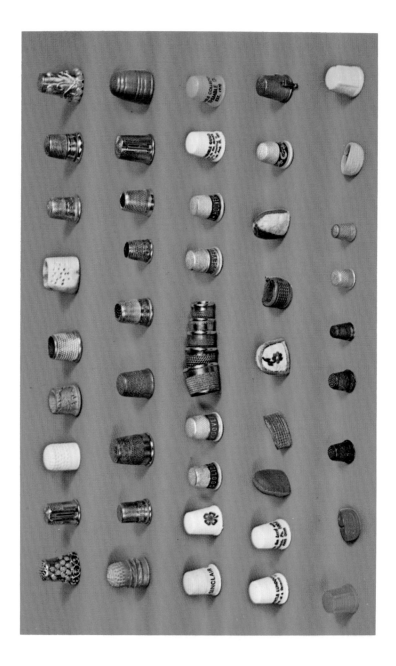

TOP ROW: (1) Mexican silver, turquoise settings. (2) Novelty nickel, thread cutter and needle threader. (3) Old ivory, top piece separate, Scrimshaw band. (4) Carved sandalwood. (5) Tailor's (or open top) thimble. (6) Eskimo thimble, reindeer horn. (7) Prudential advertising thimble, aluminum, 1904 or 1908. (8) Her Majesty thimble. (9) Mexican turquoise settings.

SECOND ROW: (1) Vegetable ivory. (2) Prudential advertising, brass, 1904 or 1908. (3) Iron, lined with brass. (4) Molded lead. (5) Brass, amethyst top. (6) Brass, open top, inscribed "Friendship". (7) Nickel with magnet on top, Germany. (8) Novelty, Made in U.S., razor and needle threader, Pat. (9) Myrtlewood thimble, custommade.

THIRD ROW: (1) Sinclair advertising thimble. Dinosaur on opposite side. (2) 4-H thimble. (3) Campaign thimble, Coolidge-Dawes. (4) Campaign thimble, Hoover-Curtis (1928). (5) Nest of thimbles. (6) Campaign thimble. Roosevelt-Garner. (7) Campaign thimble, Hoover-Home-Happiness (1928). (8) Thimble Guild, August 11, 1974. (9) Thimble Guild, Est. 1970.

FOURTH ROW: (1) Personal thimble. (2) Biblical quotation. "Serve the Lord with Gladness." (3) Korean, linenlike fabric over cardboard, handsewn. (4) Japanese, Leather ringtype, expandable. (5) Chinese tea cozy type, brocade embroidered, very old. (6) Japanese, leather-bound with plastic. (7) Korean. (8) Aluminum, horseshoes and shamrocks. (9) Brass, with needle pusher and thread cutter.

FIFTH ROW: (1) Blue plastic with posts to keep from rolling. (2) Red plastic, ring type. (3-7) Children's thimbles. (8) Pink plastic, ring type. (9) Yellow plastic with posts.

ABOVE: Gold and enamel. Tall item in third row is a nail guard.

TOP ROW: (1) Sterling with gold inlay, Celtic crosses, French. (2) Silver, gilt, enamel, Russian. (3) Silver thistle, Scotland. (4) Enamel on metal, Portrait, made in Bombay. (5) Gold with five diamonds.

SECOND ROW: Group of gold thimbles. (1) Dancing figures. (3) Raised grape.

THIRD ROW: Group of thimbles. (1) Gold band. Others are gold.

FOURTH ROW: Group of silver thimbles.

FIFTH ROW: Foreign. (1) and (2) Scandinavian. (3) Chinese. (4) Japanese. (5) Scandinavian.

All are silver, enamel, or porcelain.

All are gold and silver; note bottom center thimble with applied flower set with turquoise.

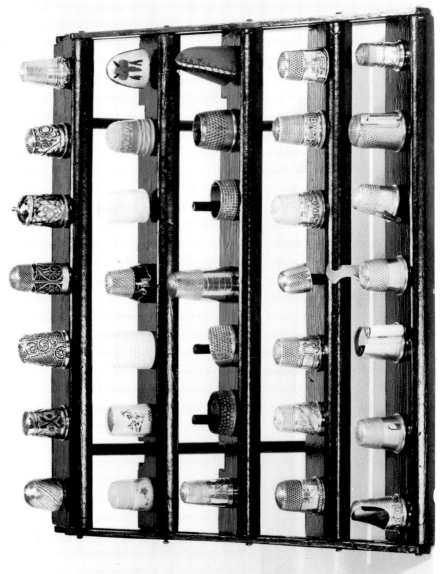

From the collection of Elizabeth Galbraith Sickels

28

TOP ROW: (1) Silver, design hand incised with punch and mallet, gilded inside, circa 1756, French (Parismarks). (2) Silver with black enamel design, nineteenth century Russian. (3) Silver, hand cut, circa 1880. (4) Silver filigree. Eighteenth century, English. (5) Niello work, cutouts in the design to catch the needle, Russian, lug on top to attach this to a chatelaine, eighteenth century. (6) Silver, hand hammered. (7) Silver, band cast and soldered to upper part, edge to edge, band shows traces of having been gilded, circa 1780, probably English—no marks.

SECOND ROW: (1) Bone, hand painted. (2) Reindeer horn with head of reindeer burned on side with hot needle, steel set in apex, Finland. (3) Beef bone, Scrimshaw work. (4) White metal with walrus ivory band hand painted black, with colored spools of thread, signed "Tita." (5) Elephant ivory, hand carved. (6) Vegetable ivory, circa 1850. (7) Silk, hand made and embroidered, twentieth century, Korean.

THIRD ROW: (1) Spun silver, circa 1780, probably English, no marks. (2) Bronze, 300 B.C., Etruscan. (3) Brass, twentieth century, Japanese. (4) Pinchbeck, steel capped, eighteenth century, probably English, no marks. (5) Brass, twentieth century, Chinese. (6) Steel, brass lined, nineteenth century. (7) Leather, hand made, twentieth century, Korean.

FOURTH ROW: (1) Silver, Columbian Exposition souvenir, "1492-1892," American. (2) Sterling, St. Augustine, Florida; souvenir bearing coat of arms and "Settled 1565," circa 1900. (3) Sterling, Salem (Mass.), souvenir bearing witch, cat, new moon and three pins on band, also 1692, circa 1892, Ketcham and McDougall. (4) Silver, hand made, circa 1750. (5) Sterling, replica of St. Louis Exposition souvenir, modern, Simons Bros. 1904. (6) Silver, Hamburg (Germany) souvenir, amethyst set in apex, gilded inside. (7) Sterling, Homestead Hotel, Hot Springs, Virginia, nineteenth century, Ketcham and McDougall.

FIFTH ROW: (1) Sterling, left hand index finger guard for hand sewing, 1868, English (London marks). (2) White metal patent thimble, thread cutter on side, American. (3) Nickel silver patent thimble, patented 1870, American, hem roller. (4) White metal "Thimble Pic" for ripping seams. Twentieth century American. (5) White metal patent thimble, needle threader on side, patented 1869, American. (6) Gilded metal patent thimble, combination sliding wire needle threader and thread cutter on side, twentieth century, American. (7) Silver, steel capped, "1854" engraved inside as well as outside.

FIRST ROW: Stone caps. (1) Jade, England. (2) Hessonite garnet (also called rose garnet), Austria. (3) Moonstone, all-over enamel, Norway. (4) Carnelian, satin gold plated, cloisonne in two shades green and white, Norway. (5) Moonstone, cloisonne in blue and white, Norway.

SECOND ROW: (1) Steel top, Sweden. (2) France. (3) U.S. Pat. Sept. 20, 1881. MKD. (4) Germany.

THIRD AND FOURTH ROWS: All Scandinavian thimbles, all with gems or stones in tops.

FIFTH ROW: All with applied motifs: (1) Viking ship. (2) Owl, modern. (3) Beehive, old Japanese. (4) Bicentennial Liberty Bell, modern. (5) Beetle with synthetic jewels.

SIXTH-ROW: (1) Tai dancer, modern. (2) Shield, probably for monogram. (3) Typical Black Hills gold in three colors, grape and leaves. (4) Great Northern Railroad goat. (5) Tai, three-headed elephant, modern.

FIRST ROW: (1) Victoria and Albert, married at St. James Palace Feb. 10, 1840. (2) Windsor Castle. (3) V (crown) R. (4) In commemoration of the Diamond Jubilee, 1831-1891, of Queen Victoria. (5) Investiture of Prince Charles at Caernarvon Castle. (6) World's Columbian Exposition 1893. (7) "Marienbad," very old, amethyst top. (8) James Walker, the London jeweler. (9) "James Walker wishes you luck." (10) Donner Pass.

SECOND ROW: (1) "Jerusalem," amber top. (2) D.A.R. (old) Daughters of American Revolution. (3) 4-H Club. (4) Black Hills gold. (5) The Embroiders' Guild of America, Inc. (6) Atlantic Cable. (7) Strawberry Bank. (8) St. Louis World's Fair, 1904. (9) Salem Witch. (10) Florida with alligator.

THIRD ROW: (1) Brass U.S. flag in color. (2) Mount Vernon. (3) Reverse side says "George Washington." (4) Madrid, Spain. (5) Fatima. (6) Christmas Bells and Holly. (7) Mistletoe. (8) Poinsettias. (9) Horse shoes and four-leaf clover. (10) Four-leaf clovers all around.

THIRD ROW: (1) Very heavy. (2) Embroidery all over, set with three rubies and three turquoise. (3) Marked 14K. (4) Pale blue enameled band. (5) English, hallmarks around bottom. (6) Platinum and gold applied flowers alternating. (7) Unusual applied decoration and engraving. (8) Very old, inside apex are numerous hallmarks (old English C instead of K) indicating 18K gold, made in Chester, England in 1805. The top is amethyst, no knurls, but engraved castles all around. (9) Black enamel in bottom decoration, very old. (10) One quite large diamond set in block of gold. (11) Turquoise sets, Aberdeen, Scotland.

FOURTH ROW: (1) Gold band, overhanging poppy or wild rose. (2) Three color "Black Hills" gold. (3) Silver, Italian or Brazil, set with green stones. (4) Niello, Russian. (5) French 18K, the "eagle's head," mark of French 18K, visible with loop. (6) Engraved band. (7) All-over lower band design in three colors of gold. (8) Applied design, lower edge engraved "Jane Udal July 28, 1885." (9) Persian 18K, newer ones 14K. (10) Diamond, rubies, sapphires in lower band.

FIRST ROW: (1) English with fifteen diamonds around base. (2-3) Set with turquoise, very old and heavy, set with four diamonds and four rubies. (4) English, 18K, six good-sized genuine emeralds, circa 1850. (5) Very heavy cloisonne in pale blue and gold, four pearls. (6) French, "Bright Cut." (7) French, scalloped border, applied trim. (8) Applied band on stippled background. (9) Russian enamel, marks visible on lower edge, "84" and "Kokashnic." (10) Early mother of pearl.

SECOND ROW: (1) Pearls and coral from Aberdeen, Scotland. (2) Platinum and gold trim. (3) Flowers in three colors of gold. (4-5) Scalloped lower edge. (6) Green gold, very heavy. (7) Gold "Cupid." (8) French, applied band, delicately designed with turquoise sets. (9) Cobalt enamel band, engraved inside Aug. 26, 1845. (10) Very old French, hand made by family goldsmith for the lady of the manor. (11) Green enamel, white dots, engraved "Bermuda."

Bottom row is all embroidery thimbles.

36

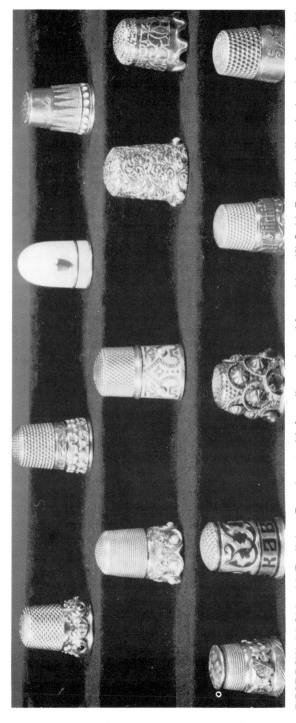

FIRST ROW: (1) Old gold, English or French, set with four diamonds and four rubies. (2) Gold, English, hallmarked on band, set with fifteen diamonds. (3) M.O.P., circa 1790. (4) Gold, the points green enamel, white enamel dots.

SECOND ROW: (1) Old gold, set with seven turquoise. (2) Cloisonne in gold, pale blue, set with pearls. (3) Gold, set with rubies and turquoise. (4) Solid gold, marked 14K.

THIRD ROW: (1) Irish, sterling, with "shamrock and harp," green or jade top. (2) Russian niello, marked "84", ladies head with veil. (3) Brazil, silver wire, set with emeralds. (4) "A Stitch in Time." (5) "Salem Witch.".

MUSEUMS

Thimbles have won recognition as memorabilia. A single item of special interest, or a large collection, may be viewed in many museums.

The following pages illustrate several collections.

BRITISH MUSEUM provided pictures of two commemorative thimbles:

Nation's Day in 1851 is depicted with an equestrian distinctly visible on the band.

Queen Victoria's coronation in 1838 is commemorated by a handsome thimble with roses, thistles and shamrocks, symbolizing England, Scotland and Ireland.

HUNT COLLECTION is shown through the courtesy of Mrs. Emily Hunt and the Washington Historical Society, Washington, Connecticut, which handles the collection.

PROCTOR COLLECTION at the Munson-Williams-Proctor Institute, Utica, New York, is represented by items from the collection of Mrs. Thomas R. Proctor and her sister, Mrs. Frederick T. Proctor. The sisters married the Proctor brothers. All were interested in collecting.

HYDE COLLECTION at Glens Falls, New York, includes the thimble collection of the late Mrs. Louis Fiske Hyde. In 1963 the Hyde Collection of paintings, sculpture, furnishings and books, assembled by Mr. and Mrs. Hyde, was opened as a museum "to promote and cultivate the study and improvement of the fine arts."

TEMPLE SQUARE MUSEUM, Salt Lake City, Utah, has a thimble used by Brigham Young, 1801-1877, to mend his tent during the westward trek of the Mormons.

AMERICAN SWEDISH MUSEUM in Philadelphia has a record of brass thimbles discovered at several depths of excavation at the site of Printz Hall on Tinicum Island where a Swedish colony

COMMEMORATIVE. Made to mark Queen Victoria's coronation in 1838. Silver. Oval medallion of Queen Victoria surrounded by thistles, roses, and shamrocks. (Used through the courtesy of the Department of Medieval and Later Antiquities, The British Museum, London.)

COMMEMORATIVE. "Exhibition of All Nations 1851." Silver. Engraved with large building in background and figures, one equestrian, in foreground. (Used through the courtesy of the Department of Medieval and Later Antiquities, The British Museum, London.)

existed from 1638 to 1655. The thimbles are not available for viewing nor is it known where they are presently preserved.

THOMAS JEFFERSON MEMORIAL FOUNDATION, Charlottesville, Virginia, has three silver thimbles which belonged to members of the Jefferson family at Monticello. One is initialed V.J.T., for Virginia Jefferson Trist.

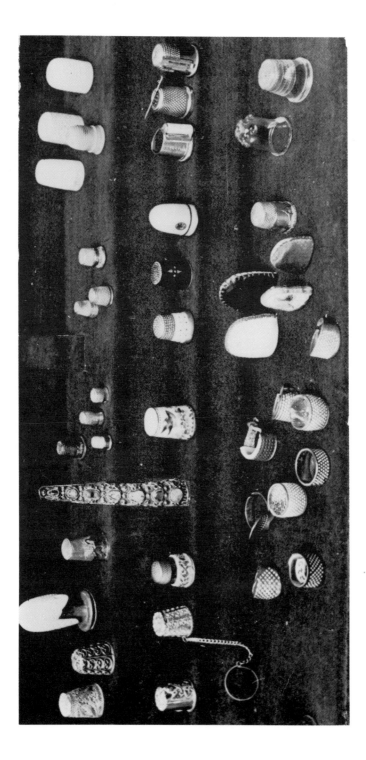

The Hunt Collection

Washington Historical Society
Washington, Connecticut

MANY NATIONS are represented in these thimbles of diverse designs, varying sizes, and assorted materials in the collection of Mrs. William M. Hunt. (Photo by Peter Adams, The Waterbury Republican and American.)

TOP ROW: (1) Tehran. (2) Salzburg. (3) Ivory, Eider duck, hand-made in Labrador. (4) French fable, Fox and Stork, tall and tapering with square knurling. (5-6) Children's thimbles. (7-8) Charms. (9, 10, 11) Children's thimbles, very old. (12) Ivory, Chinese, "Year of the Tiger," one of a series. (13, 14) Vegetable ivory. (15) Beef bone, scrimshaw border.

SECOND ROW: (1) Thailand, heavy silver, plain sides with applied figures of gods, also one on apex, no knurlings. (2) Istanbul, raised all over design instead of knurlings, small design on rim, attached chain and ring. (3) Petit point border. (4) Chinese finger guard. (5) English porcelain, old. (6) Porcelain, old. (7) Tortoise shell, top gold plate, probably foreign, possibly American, circa 1875. (8) Mother-of-pearl, gold medallion inset with enamel flower, two gold stripes on band, French, nineteenth century. (9) Nickel silver hem roller, "Pat. 1870," half open except for rim and a band around top, ivory roller. (10) Magnetic top. (11) Thread cutter and needle threader.

THIRD ROW: (1) Group of nine ring-type thimbles: Japan, Hong Kong, Saigon, Okinawa (third in group). (2) Group of four "tea cozy" type thimbles, plastic or embroidered silk, Japan and Korea. (3) Wide band design of church and little house and two birds. (4) Blown glass, Florida. (5) Corning glass.

PROCTOR COLLECTION

Munson-Williams-Proctor Institute
Utica, New York

THESE THIMBLES are from the collection of Mrs. Thomas R. Proctor and Mrs. Frederick T. Proctor.

TOP ROW: (1) Carved thimble edged in gold. (2) Hand sewn pigskin thimble, double thickness.

SECOND ROW: (1) Silver thimble, Simons Bros., decorated with gadroon edge and band of wave pattern. (2) Silver thimble. Simons Bros., band with cupids and garland in relief. (3) Gold thimble, Simons Bros., 14K decorative band set with turquoise. (4) Silver thimble, Ketcham and McDougall, sterling, plain band with rococo edge and body. (5, 6) Two silver thimbles, Ketcham and McDougall, sterling, decorative border with legend "Salem/1692" pictures witch and other symbols.

THIRD ROW: (1) Silver thimble with scene decorating body of thimble, marked, lion passant, crowned leopard and "b", 1737-38. (2) Silver thimble with shell-like decorative motif, circa 1870. (3) Silver thimble with spray of seed pearls and blue glass, marked "RO", "J", nineteenth century. (4) Purple enamel thimble with white stone top, marked 925. (5) Bronze thimble, possibly ancient Roman. (6) Silver thimble in child's size, engraved "Rachel," marked "F. & Co.", circa 1850.

FOURTH ROW: (1) Silver thimble with enamel oval painted with a cat, marked "935". (2, 3) Pair of silver thimbles with decorated band, set with red and green stones, smaller of two inscribed "Edinburgh," each marked with number 2025. (4) Silver thimble with projecting decorative band extending out from thimble, mosaic-type design of birds and flowers made with enamel colored chips. (5) Silver thimble with purple glass top, engraved design, inscribed "ODDE", "835". (5) Silver thimble with filigree edging below indentation, possibly late eighteenth century.

FIFTH ROW: (1,2) Pair of silver thimbles with band of turquoise stones. (3) Gold thimble engraved with monogram "HAW" (Williams or Watson family), very thin with several holes, early nineteenth century. (4) Silver thimble with initials "HEM" (belonged to Helen Elizabeth Munson), circa 1820. (5) Silver thimble with red glass top, Russian mark "84", inscribed "Na pamyat," meaning souvenir or keepsake, circa 1890. (6) Niello decorated thimble with Russian mark "84", Vine design and inscription "Kavkaz" meaning Caucasus.

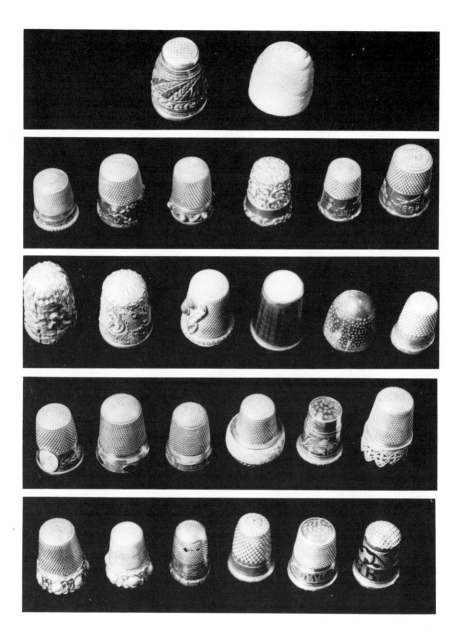

PROCTOR COLLECTION (continued)

FIRST ROW: (1) Sterling silver thimble, Ketcham and McDougall, Decorative band has sprigs of blossoms. (2) Sterling silver thimble, Ketcham and McDougall, decorative band with legend "Hey Diddle Diddle," pictures cat and fiddle and cow jumping over the moon (from the nursery rhyme), after 1875. (3) Sterling silver thimble, Ketcham and McDougall, decorative band with legend "Old Stone Mill—Newport R.I.," after 1875. (4) Sterling silver thimble, Ketcham and McDougall, decorative band with legend "Richfield Springs N.Y.," after 1875. (5) Silver thimble with band of red, white and blue enamel, Simons Bros.

SECOND ROW: (1) Souvenir thimble of Queen Victoria's Jubilee "1837 in commemoration 1897," pictures head of Queen Victoria and monogram, marked "D&F". (2) Silver thimble with applied enamel shield with scene and inscription, "Foro Umberto Palermo". (3) Souvenir silver thimble with applied enamel shield, inscribed "Praig". (4) Souvenir silver thimble with applied oval enamel shield picturing hooded figure holding stein, inscribed "Munchen." (5) Souvenir silver thimble with "Quebec" in large letters, inscribed "G. Seiffert" on inside.

THIRD ROW: (1) Silver thimble with "Menton" in large letters, marked with diamond shaped lozenge and initial J. (2) Silver thimble inset with red glass top, inscribed "Heidelberg." (3) Silver thimble, enamelled band painted with lake scene, inscribed "Geneve." (4) Silver thimble, green glass or stone top. Inscribed "Bergin Erindring." (5) Silver thimble, purple glass top, band of scrolls, with scalloped edge, engraved "Stockholm," marked below band with "W" in trefoil.

FOURTH ROW: (1) Silver thimble inscribed "Souvenir St. Augustine, Florida," pictures Fort Marion, Old Cathedral and old city gate, Patented 1881. (2) Silver thimble with design of raised flowers, shield inscribed "Atlanta/ '05." (3) Silver thimble with rococo design and shield, engraved "Helsingfors," marked with crown, RM R4 and number 818, made in two pieces. (4) Gold thimble with white glass top, band of white stones and band of blue enamel, engraved "Throndhjem," marked "925". (5) Silver thimble, with brown stone top, faceted rim, bright-cut border, engraved "Newquay" on inside rim, marked "J.S.", an anchor, lion and "i", Birmingham, 1908.

FIFTH ROW: (1) Silver thimble with enamel yellow and red shield, surmounted by crown. Inscribed "Baden-Baden." (2) Silver thimble with oval shield picturing bird, inscribed "Neran." (3) Metal thimble with thread cutter, inscribed "Duke, Pat. May 15, 1900/9". (4) Clear cut glass thimble. (5) Amber colored cut glass thimble.

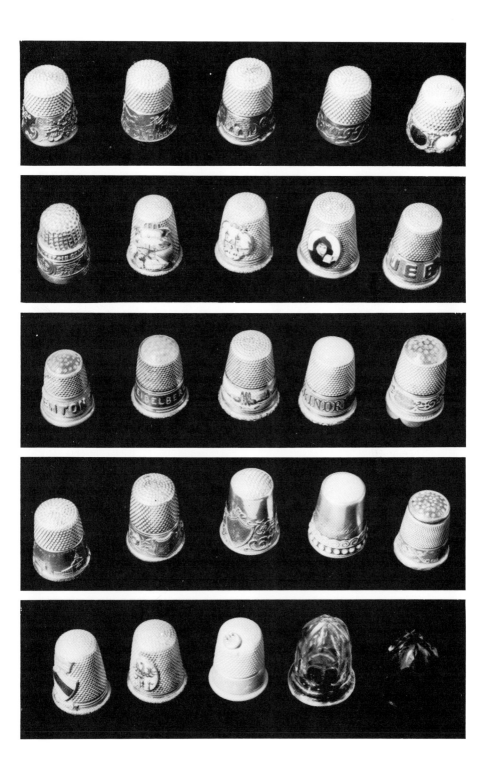

45

PROCTOR COLLECTION (continued)

FIRST ROW: (1) Silver thimble with niello inscription, Napamyat," meaning souvenir or keepsake; Russian mark, "84" only half visible; probably before 1890, lettering style older and single word earlier form. (2) Black thimble with embroidered cover, accompanying note reads "Puerto Rico, Mr. Proctor." (3) Silver thimble with green enamel band decorated with gold stars and butterflies; marked with "A", a mark used on silver from Vienna in the 1870s. (4) Silver thimble with green glass top and decorated band of various symbols, star, cross, heart and anchor; marked with "A". (5) Silver thimble with blue enamelled anchors.

SECOND ROW: (1) Metal thimble with dolphins around border. (2) Silver thimble with purple glass top, raised vine design and shield shaped panel, marked with "a". (3) Silver thimble with protruding hollow cylinder on side, probably for pushing large needles. (4) White ceramic thimble edged in gold and painted with flowers, French, eighteenth century. (5) Pale pink ceramic thimble edged in gold and painted with pink roses, French, eighteenth century.

THIRD ROW: (1) Gold washed thimble with cloisonne enamel design, Russian mark. (2) Silver thimble with purple glass top, decorative band of open work in diamond pattern, Russian mark "84". (3) Tortoise shell thimble with silver cap, decorated with coat of arms flanked by unicorn and figure, inscribed "Piercy's Patent." (4) Silver thimble with black design of island and boats, South Sea island scene. (5) Silver thimble with green glass top, art nouveau type design, circa 1900.

FOURTH ROW: (1) Silver thimble with art nouveau type design of leaves, marked with impressed "G" in circle, circa, 1900. (2) Silver thimble with art nouveau type design of flowers on long stems. (3) Silver thimble with design of indentations, marked "Pat. 10" inside a rectangle, silver cap broken loose from body. (4) Silver thimble with brilliantly cut indentations which sparkle, marked "Pat. 9". (5) Silver thimble with quatrefoil design indentations and decorative band of lilies of the valley, marked with "G" inside a circle.

FIFTH ROW: (1) Silver thimble with design of leaves around band, engraved with initials "MH", circa 1800. (2) Silver thimble decorated with two large stylized flowers and scalloped border, circa 1800. (3) Gold thimble made in two pieces, indentations mixed with stars, design of tulips in four panels, eighteenth century. (4) Silver thimble with all-over rococo design, circa 1790. (5) Gold thimble stamped with animal, bell and Paris 3rd gold standard mark (1819-1838); chased design in grid pattern with petal design on top of thimble, border band of different colored gold in leaf pattern.

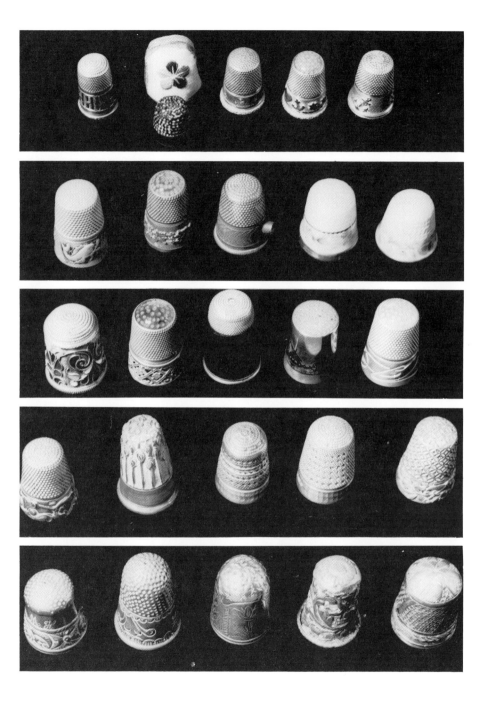

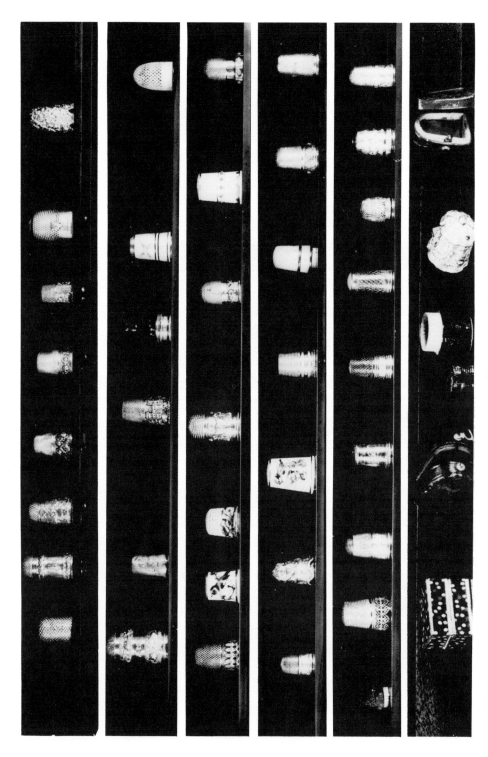

HYDE COLLECTION
Glens Falls, New York

HYDE HOUSE in Glens Falls, New York, was originally a home but eventually became a setting for The Hyde Collection of painting, sculpture, furniture, and books assembled by Mr. and Mrs. Louis Fiske Hyde. The thimbles were collected by Mrs. Hyde.

TOP ROW: (1) Gold, English, eighteenth century "High Standard Period." (2) Gold, Classic Period, circa 1860. (3) Gold, French, nineteenth century, Classic Period. (4) Gold, English or French, 1775-1800. (5) Gold, English, late eighteenth century. (6) Silver, American, circa 1850. (7) Silver, Dutch, early nineteenth century. (8) Italian, seventeenth century, solid gold.

SECOND ROW: (1) Gold, French, 1800. (2) Classic style, 1770-1825. (3) Silver, American, 1764, possibly done by Paul Revere. (4) Silver, English Victorian, mid-nineteenth century, commemorative thimble, small amethyst scent bottle screws into thimble.(5) Pale green enamel, English, circa 1850. (6) Ivory, Beehive shaped, mid to late eighteenth century.

THIRD ROW: (1) Silver, late rococo. French, 1760. (2) Porcelain, French, nineteenth century. (3) Porcelain, German, eighteenth century. (4) Gold, Italian, eighteenth century. (5) Gold, French, early 1700s. (6) Porcelain,

English Derby. 1815. (7) Gold, English. circa 1800, six turquoise around bottom.

FOURTH ROW: (1) Silver, English, circa 1800. (2) Gold, Italian, circa 1760. (3) Porcelain, Royal Worcester. English. circa 1890. (4) Rose gold, English, circa 1875, amethyst tops thimble. (5) Mother-of-pearl, French. circa 1780-1790. (6) Gold, French, circa 1800, turquoise around thimble. (7) Gold, English, nineteenth century, topped with amethyst.

FIFTH ROW: (1) Bronze, Gallo-Roman, late second to early third century. (2) Silver, French, eighteenth century, inlaid gold in shape of crosses. (3) Silver, English, circa 1800, steel top. (4) Silver, English. circa 1800, Method of design called Niello. (5) Silver, English, eighteenth century. (6) Silver, English, 1800, green enamel over a guilloche, topped with a moonstone. (7) Silver, English, early nineteenth century. (8) Silver, English, eighteenth century. (9) Silver, English, early 1800s.

SIXTH ROW: Thimble Holders: (1) Cardboard, gilt and polka-dotted paper covering; inside inscribed "E. Fiechter/ Goldschmied/ Bijoutier/ Interlaken." (2) Thimble shaped brown leather case, bottom hinge, hook and eye top, velvet and satin lined. (3) Round wooden case, green cover. (4) Gold, ornate case, fleur-de-lys pattern, button lever clasp, top with loop for chain. (5) Thimble shaped red case with satin lining.

IDENTIFYING THIMBLES

One of the most challenging problems that faces collectors is dating thimbles. Records of early makers are scarce.

Thimble collectors are pioneering in the identification of marks on thimbles and the nucleus of a calendar of dates is being established.

However, a few marks which appear on plentiful thimbles elude identification.

Many fine old thimbles are unmarked which makes identification difficult.

Reference books on marks of silversmiths rarely include thimble-makers. Small companies making thimbles were seldom included in compilations of identifying data, probably because thimbles were considered to be unimportant. For this reason, research is slow in substantiating marks existing on thimbles.

On holders with matching thimbles, the maker may appear on the holder but not on the thimble.

It is known that silversmiths produced custom-made articles, especially small items such as thimbles, which may not bear a mark.

Old catalogs, newspaper advertisements, magazines, inventories, and patent papers are a few sources of information about thimbles.

Thimbles may be identified by hallmarks, trademarks (maker's mark), or punchmarks.

Punchmarks

Early American silversmiths used a punchmark, also called a touchmark, to identify their work, especially when there were a number of smiths working in a shop. A punchmark is a small impression on silver of a letter, animal, or symbol to identify the maker. These marks are found mostly on larger pieces of silver, but some thimbles were so marked. Few of the actual touchmark tools exist because it was customary to destroy a silversmith's punchmark at the time of his death.

Trademarks

Trademarks may be found on top, at the side, inside, or almost any place on a thimble where there is space for it. Some trademarks are registered.

Patent dates on thimbles do not necessarily indicate the date of manufacture as patented thimbles may be produced for many years after the original patent date.

Prior to 1830, silver was made to order, the customer providing coin silver and dealing directly with the silversmith.

Classifying by Style

As a rule of thumb, unmarked thimbles may be classified according to the approximate period the style of ornament was popular. This cannot be a bonafide placement because thimbles may have been ordered according to personal preference rather than the current fashion.

Periods of Style

Fifteenth Century, Renaissance: Profuse, lavish design. Reign of Queen Elizabeth I.

1697-1720, High Standard: Silver was softer. More refined lines were used in flutings, spirals and foliage.

1720-1770, Rococo Period: Silver was returned to standard content and lavish all-over patterns, scrolls, flowers and ribbons were in vogue.

1770-1825, Classic Period: Greek and Roman designs became popular, influenced by excavations at Herculaneum and Pompeii. Drapery, bead borders, foliage, fruit and Greek key motifs were popular.

Hall marks on British Silver

Over 600 years ago, a system of hallmarking silver was instituted in England. The British hallmark is a reliable symbol of considerable chronological value.

Prior to 1780, thimbles and other small silver items were exempt from hallmarking.

From 1784 until 1890, the reigning Sovereign's Head in profile, as a fifth mark on silver, indicated an excise duty collected by assay offices for the Inland Revenue.

From 1790 until 1837, the Sovereign's Head faced to the right.

From 1837 until 1890, the Sovereign's Head faced to the left.

Since the McKinley Act of 1891, all thimbles made for export to the United States have been marked "England" or "Made in England."

Since 1890, English silver has four marks, the maker's mark, mark of origin, assay mark, and date letter. The maker's mark consists of the initials of the maker or firm registered at an assay office. It is possible to identify the maker by referring to the assay office.

There are now only four assay offices in Great Britain: Birmingham (Anchor), London (Leopard's Head), Sheffield (Crown), and Edinburgh (Castle of Three Towers).

To identify hallmarks on a thimble, find first the maker's mark and city of origin so that a table of date letters for that assay office may be consulted. Tables are available in standard books of reference and in convenient pamphlets.

Lion Passant indicates sterling quality.

The lion's head erased and "Brittania" was used only from 1697 to 1720 to indicate a higher standard of silver. These marks are extremely rare.

An old thimble definitely dated by hallmarks affords exaltation to the collector.

Japan

Ivory thimbles of Japan are sometimes marked in a twelve-year cycle of naming years for animals in the following order: tiger, rabbit, dragon, serpent, horse, sheep, monkey, fowl, dog, boar, rat, cow. Thus, going forward or backward, every twelfth year has the same symbolic animal.

America

Before the turn of the century in America, there were about half a dozen manufacturers with thimble making devices who produced thimbles in large quantities:

> Goldsmith Stern and Company (previously known as Stern Bros. and Company.)
>
> Carter Gough Company.
>
> Ketcham and McDougall
>
> Simons Bros.
>
> Untermeyer-Robbins Company.
>
> Waite-Thresher Company.
>
> Webster Company.

Their marks appear on many older thimbles in collections. All thimbles were of excellent quality and craftsmanship.

Common Marks

Following are marks more commonly found on early thimbles and/or holders:

Thomas S. Brogan
New York, N. Y.

 Charles Horner
England

Gabler Bros.
Germany
Some slight variations.
See Proctor thimble tops.

 Stern Bros. Co.
New York, N. Y.
(Later with Goldsmith Stern Company.)

Goldsmith Stern Company
New York, N. Y.

 Ketcham & McDougall
Brooklyn, N. Y.

53

Simons Bros.
Philadelphia, Pa.
Many variations.

H. Muhr Sons
Philadelphia, Pa.

Untermeyer-Robbins & Company

Webster Company
North Attelboro, Mass.

Waite-Thresher Co.
Providence, R.I.
(Early mark a star.)
Barker Manufacturing Company
(Also used star.)
(Later part of Waite-Thresher Company)

Waite-Thresher Company
(Later mark)
(When Waite-Thresher Company went
out of business, Simons Bros.
bought designs)

Inscriptions Found on Thimbles

It is no wonder that many treasured thimbles still exist because of sentiments inscribed, such as:

Fare well
Friendship
From a Friend
A Keepsake
A Token of Regard
Forget-Me-Not
Remember Me
I will remember thee

"Remember Me," "Forget-Me-Not," or "Fare Well" embossed on a thimble generations ago may still evoke appreciation of the donor and receiver. There was something final about farewells when the thimble was to be carried overseas in a sailing vessel or across the continent in a covered wagon.

Thimbles reigned when quilting bees were social events, disseminating skills and news and understanding. There were no idle hands. There was responsibility. There were satisfactions. There is therapy in thimbles.

RARE PORCELAIN THIMBLE

Porcelain is a general term used for fine earthenware with a translucent base covered with transparent glass.

Marco Polo described porcelain in stories of his travels in the Orient about 1285 A.D. Later, trading vessels bringing specimens to Europe created a demand. Many potteries attempted to imitate porcelain without success. The earthenware produced was crude by comparison.

In about 1710, Johann Bottger discovered a method of making fine porcelain, and Augustus the Strong of Saxony established a factory. The smooth surface of porcelain served artists well. The porcelains of Meissen became famous.

Meissen Thimble

The thimble opposite, circa 1730, was sold at auction by Christie Galleries, London, in 1969. The price was $3,780.

This one-half inch tall thimble was painted in the famous Herold workshop at Meissen (Saxony) early in the eighteenth century with a continuous harbour scene. Around the band is a miniature chinoiserie scene with six ships, thirty figures, six bales of cotton and a barrel. This particular thimble is also of great interest because of its castellated shape. Most porcelain thimbles have straight edges.

Johann Gregorious Herold (Horoldt), born 1696, a color-chemist, was Director of Painting at the Meissen factory from 1722 until at least 1750, beginning what came to be called the Herold era. He evolved the Meissen decorative style.

Herold painted harbour scenes, with merchants loading ships, depicting activities along the wharves. Trading with the Orient was an important endeavor of the time. Every harbour was the scene of much activity.

Chinoiserie is a style of scenic decoration fundamentally Chinese. Chinamen performing varied activities were painted in miniature. Several miniaturists are believed to have painted figures or landscapes on one piece in assembly fashion.

The famous crossed swords porcelain mark, derived from the arms of Saxony, was first used at Meissen under Augustus the Strong.

Porcelain thimbles were made at several English potteries, Worcester, Spode, Minton, Derby, Chelsea, and others.

Porcelain thimbles are an art form, beautiful but rarely practicable.

THE RARE ONE!

A group of fine porcelain thimbles.

ATLANTIC CABLE THIMBLE

A silver thimble now in the Science Museum, London, served in 1866 to complete a stupendous engineering project which had been attempted twice before without success.

Silver thimbles known to collectors as Atlantic Cable thimbles deserve special mention. There are no marks to identify the maker. During the period prior to and after 1866, marks were not required on many small articles, including thimbles.

Variations exist in the size and height of the Atlantic Cable thimble. At least one was perforated in the scallops around the heavy edge. A stem and floral design zigzag around a wide band. All variations of the Atlantic Cable thimble are identified as having been made by the same silversmith. Such heavy applied edges were rare.

The tiny thimble was used during testing of the early submarine telegraph cable across the Atlantic. After several unsuccessful attempts, two cables were laid in 1866 between Valencia in Ireland and White Stand Bay, Newfoundland.

Latimer Clark, who went to Valencia to test the cable for the Atlantic Company, arranged for the Newfoundland ends to be connected, thus forming an unbroken length of 3,700 miles in circuit. Current from an electric battery was sent through the cable from Ireland to Newfoundland and back again. The battery used for this experiment was created by Mr. Clark in the following manner.

He borrowed a thimble from Miss Emily Fitzgerald, daughter of the Knight of Kerry upon whose land in Valencia the cable terminated. The Knight of Kerry had evinced great interest in and offered every assistance in furtherance of the Atlantic Cable enterprise from the beginning.

A miniature cell was created consisting only of a few drops of acid and a fragment of zinc in the silver thimble. By this primitive agency, Mr. Clark succeeded in passing a current from the miniature electric cell, conveying signals through the breadth of the Atlantic Ocean in a little more than a second. The current from this improvised cell was sufficient to give full and clear deflections on the "Mirror Speaking Galvanometer," which had been recently devised by Professor W. Thomson, later Lord Kelvin, who played an active part in the transatlantic cable-laying.

The event was fully described in The Illustrated London News of September 8, 1866.

The use of the thimble is included also in a biography of Sir Charles Tilston Bright.

The thimble used in this historic experiment was presented to the ScienceMuseum by R. B. Fitzgerald, Esq., a nephew of the late Miss Emily.

The development of communication from primitive signals to satellite earth stations must include the transatlantic telegraph in which a thimble played an important part.

The first public message was sent by Queen Victoria to the President of the United States.

Let it not be forgotten that the first signals were sent across the Atlantic Ocean through the use of Emily Fitzgerald's thimble.

A PIECE of the Atlantic Cable is pictured with the thimble used to send the first message. (Photograph through courtesy "British Crown Copyright, Science Museum, South Kensington, London.)

JAPANESE SEWING

The Yubi-nuki

The Japanese thimble is called a yubi-nuki, literally "finger-put-through." This is a ring-type, expandable band about a half-inch wide, made of leather or metal. Ends of the leather are tied together with thread, the length of the thread between the ends being adjusted to the circumference of the finger which will use it. Ends of metal thimbles may be bent closer together or spread apart as needed.

All sewing in Japan was done by hand until the more or less recent advent of the sewing machine, as in other countries. Much fine work is still done by hand in Japan. Clothing is usually made of thin silk or cotton. Tiny, even running stitches seam parts together. Formerly, every-day wear was ripped apart for washing and sewed together again afterward. In colder seasons, an inner lining was placed between the layers.

It will be conceded by some, after practicing, that using the yubi-nuki, Japanese fashion, is an efficient method of sewing. Very little arm motion is required. No thimbles are used in blind stitching or hemming. Some palm pushers are used for very heavy work.

Mrs. Chiyoko Oda, who demonstrated the method described below, learned to sew in a Japanese school at the age of eight. Teachers enforced strict rules regarding size of stitches and increase of speed in working. Much practice was required to achieve perfection. Left-handed sewing was not permitted.

Method

The thimble is worn between the first and second joints of the middle finger of the right hand, with indentations outward.

A short threaded needle is held between the thumb and index finger of the right hand, which also grips the fabric, with the thimble firmly pressing against the end of the needle. The thimble remains in this position against the needle.

The left hand holds the material four or five inches to the left as the right hand weaves the needle in and out, gathering evenly spaced shirring on the needle. The left hand assists with a slightly forward and backward tautness of the material as the needle proceeds along the seam.

When there are ten or twelve stitches along the needle, the left index finger and thumb grasp the tip of the needle and the material, holding them taut. (Grasping the tip of the needle with the left hand is not practiced by more experienced sewers.)

The right hand then removes the thimble from the end of the needle FOR THE FIRST TIME and pulls the material to the right along the thread, revealing short, even stitches. Repeat the procedure.

Japanese women sew 100 stitches a minute. A garment can be made by hand in one day.

Actually, by the Japanese method, material is pulled onto the thread. In other methods, the thread is pulled through the material.

Sewing with the yubi-nuki can be challenging. Used by a practiced seamstress, the method seems more efficient than that used in other countries.

GABLER BROTHERS FACTORY

The Gabler Brothers thimble factory of Schorndorf, Germany, in operation from 1824 until 1962, exported millions of thimbles annually.

In March 1807, Johann Ferdinand Gabler, a silversmith, wrote in his diary that he had designed a practical thimble that could be sold for a reasonable price. It is known that he subsequently made a device that could make thimbles by mass production. Thus the business which was to thrive for 125 years was started.

The sons of Johann Ferdinand Gabler later took over the business, moving the plant to a picturesque water-operated mill in Schorndorf, Germany.

This was the only thimble factory in the world. Thimbles were made of gold, silver, steel, brass and other metals in 14 sizes. Thimbles were exported to countries around the world. The factory closed in 1962.

Thimbles by Gebruder Gabler are of excellent quality and beautiful design. The trademark, an eight-petalled medallion on top of the thimble, is one which may have been used by ladies in former days to seal a letter.

DETAILS OF A GABLER THIMBLE.

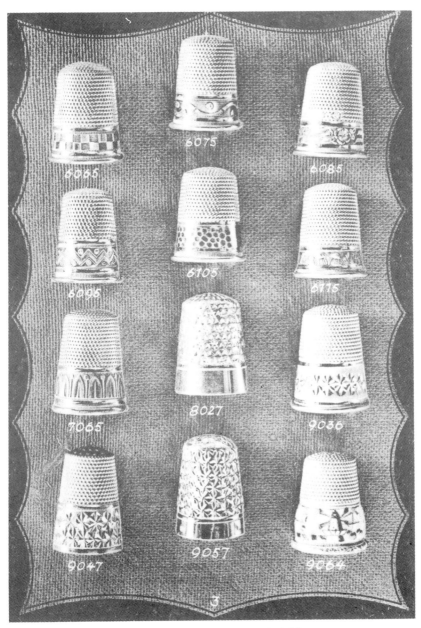

PLATE FROM A GABLER CATALOG.

63

JUST IN PROPORTION to the wisdom you display in placing your supply of Prudential thimbles, will be the measure of your success in securing signatures on Prudential Industrial applications. Use both thimbles and "apps" so that they will produce large results.

ADVERTISING THIMBLES

Advertising thimbles are among new-found interests in collecting.

Thimbles have a homey appeal and are seldom discarded. There is always room for another small thimble in a machine drawer or sewing basket, so advertisers may reap attention over a long period.

Collectors of campaign thimbles delve into history for data on Hoover, Coolidge, Roosevelt, and local booster club candidates. Campaign thimbles were made by the tens of thousands in various media.

Campaign Thimbles

The "Hoover-Home-Happiness" and "Hoover-Curtis" thimbles were used freely in the presidential campaign of 1928. Two of these thimbles are a part of memorabilia of Herbert Hoover, relating to his life and times at the Herbert Hoover Presidential Library, West Branch, Iowa.

Dinosaur Symbol

Sinclair Oil Company, now part of Atlantic-Richfield Company, formerly advertised with plastic thimbles depicting the dinosaur trademark. The thimbles are no longer available. Collectors who have one are likely to retain it. What other advertiser would use a dinosaur?

Prudential Thimbles

Probably the most plentiful old advertising thimbles are the Prudential thimbles inscribed "The Prudential Insurance Co. of America" or "The Prudential Insurance Co. of America Made in USA". The Company had one million of these thimbles made in 1904 for distribution to agents. In 1908 another million thimbles were distributed. Old records do not indicate which thimble was ordered first. It is interesting to note that most of these old thimbles in collections are in excellent condition. They are made of a heavy brass which takes a fine polish.

Aluminum Prudential thimbles are less plentiful and may not be of 1904 or 1908 vintage.

Present day gimmicks, gadgets, and costly television advertising will be hard pressed to surpass the record of the Prudential advertising thimble, still serving the company and the users well.

DISPLAY CASES

VICTORIAN FRAME

A fine collection deserves display cases which afford easy access to items on view every day.

Innovative systems of organizing or displaying a collection of thimbles are fascinating.

Cabinets used by dentists, architects and jewelers are adaptable to collections. Spool cases and printer's type drawers are favorites because of usable partitions in the drawers.

More specialized arrangements may be displayed in unique under-glass,

VITRINE

CUSTOM WALL FRAME

on-constant-view adaptations of old clocks, picture frames, vitrines, and custom-made originals.

The true collector adapts display cases with care, keeping to the original appearance as much as possible.

Most cases are dustproof. Many are lined with Pacific cloth, a fabric treated for use in tarnish-proof silver chests.

Doors should be kept tightly closed. Silver will not tarnish without circulation of air.

Some collectors prefer to display only part of a collection at one time in a small decorative arrangement.

A collection soon outgrows convenient organization. Clutter is the result. In reverse, a collection may establish efficiency in habits. A place should be reserved for duplicate items to trade.

When most convenient space is filled, the time has come to trade duplicates—or buy another case.

CLOCK CASE

CORTICELLI SILK CABINET

SPOOL CABINET

GLOSSARY

alabaster: A whitish, fine-grained variety of gypsum. Alabaster is translucent. Onyx is not.

alexandrite: Green stone which shows a red color by transmitted or artificial light. Sometimes used for thimble tops.

bright-cut: A style of wide-cut engraving in which the slashes remain bright when the article is polished.

campaign: Campaign thimbles, usually aluminum or plastic, are used for promotion in election campaigns. These are also called political thimbles.

chinoiserie: Ornamentation and craftsmanship influenced by Oriental design, popular during the eighteenth century.

cloisonne: Enamelling process in which colors are separated by divisions of silver or gold wire.

commemorative: Thimble issued in commemoration of a notable event.

continental: Continental silver. 800, 825, 830 and other figures in the 800s represent that portion of silver with a portion of alloy equal to 1000 parts. These specifications were used by several European countries.

Damascene: Decorated with inlaid work of precious metals, more frequently gold. A technique for decoration. One metal is encrusted onto another. A triangular cut is opened in the base metal and gold or silver is hammered into the groove.

embroidery: Thimbles with a fancy all-over pattern on sides and top were designated "embroidery" thimbles.

enamel: A colored glass to which metal oxides have been added for color. Enamels are fused to the surface of a metal.

engraving: A method of cutting lines into a metal by use of a graver.

etui: A small ornamental case, often elegant, fitted with scissors, needles, thimbles, thread, and other sewing necessities.

filigree: A metal work in which wires of silver and gold are applied in decorative patterns.

gutta percha: Rubberlike substance from juice of trees. Some hard rubber thimbles are believed to be gutta percha.

hall mark: English mark stamped on gold or silver articles to attest purity, comprised of (1) Monarch's mark, (2) Maker's mark, (3) Assayer's mark, and (4) Date mark.

hussy: (Contraction of "housewife," see Webster.) Handy sewing kit. So-called around the turn of the century.

impressed: Stamped on body.

incised: Drawn by hand.

industrial: (Also called occupational or commercial thimbles.) Used for specialized work. Sailor's palm, cobbler's thimble, saddlemaker's thimble, rugmaker's thimble, and many types of thimbles adapted to heavy work.

knurling: Indentations on the side and top of a thimble. Plain indentations (or dimples), square, waffle, diamond, are some varieties.

Louis XV edge: Irregular scroll-type curved edge on some thimbles. Used by at least two manufacturers.

marcasite: Iron sulphide. Faceted by mechanical process in gem-like manner.

Mauchline: A type of wood folk art made at Mauchline, Scotland, in the first half of the nineteenth century, commonly of elm or pine. Boxes and covers were incised or painted in black. Scenes and verses were popular decorations. Thimble holders were made of Mauchline ware.

Mother-of-pearl: Irridescent, internal layer of various mollusk shells, as pearl oysters, used for small articles. Distinguished from shell which is not irridescent.

niello: A design engraved deeply on silver and then filled with a black substance, sulphides of lead, silver, or copper. The process was used extensively in Russia. Dates to 1500 B.C.

open-end: Also called tailor's thimble. Smaller open-end thimbles used mostly by women are called quilting thimbles. These are used from the side, leaving the fingertip free to feel the material.

Pacific silvercloth: Trade name for a fabric treated to prevent tarnish. Used to line silver chests. Sold in department stores.

pewter: Dull, gray alloy of tin and lead.

pierced: Perforated in a decorative motif.

pinchbeck: Alloy of copper and zinc, about 80 parts copper to 17 zinc. Used during eighteenth century for inexpensive jewelry, including thimbles. When polished, pinchbeck resembles gold but does not retain polish. Named for Christopher Pinchbeck, London watchmaker.

political: (See campaign thimbles.)

punchmark: A small stamp on metal objects to identify the maker. Used by early silversmiths.

quilting thimble: (See open-end thimbles.)

repousse: Design produced in relief by hammering from the reverse side.

rococo: A style of decoration based on shell and rock shapes in vogue during the eighteenth century.

Russian: Russian silver is identified by the figures 84, 88, and 91, indicating the Russian specifications of 840/1000, 880/1000, and 910/1000 with alloy.

sandalwood: A sweet-smelling wood from several Asiatic trees used for carving thimbles. Sandalwood thimbles were believed to discourage moths in the sewing pouch.

scrimshaw: Name given to etching pictures on bone, teeth, and tusks, originally by sailors during long voyages. Scrimshaw thimbles were made for wives or sweethearts. Scrimshaw is sometimes described as the only true American folk art.

shagreen: Untanned leather made from skins of animals, covered with small granulations by pressing seeds in the hair side when moist. Usually dyed green. Used for thimbles in Ireland.

souvenir: Souvenir thimbles are designed as a scenic memento of a place.

sterling: Sterling on a thimble indicated 925 parts silver to 75 parts alloy. This is the standard for sterling.

tailor's thimble: (See open-end.)

tortoise shell: Mottled yellow and brown shell of some turtles used in inlaying.

touchmark: (See Punchmark.)

trademark: A symbol used by a manufacturer or dealer to identify products. Usually registered.

vegetable ivory: The tagua or coroza palm nut has been used by South American natives for centuries in carving tribal ornaments. Thimbles of so-called vegetable ivory come in various shades of tan or brown, decorated with carvings, usually in a matching holder.

HOMESPUN HINTS

Old almanacs, household magazines, and cookbooks contain homespun methods which may be adaptable to thimbles.

The prick of a hot needle on the inside of a thimble may indicate what it is made of.

Alabaster is translucent. Onyx is not.

To clean small brass articles, boil in equal parts of raw apples and rhubarb.

Camphor kept with silver prevents tarnish.

Celluloid smells like camphor.

Horn smells like burning feathers or meat cooking.

Gutta percha smells like rubber.

Jade: A drop of water on real jade will not run. If the drop spreads, the material is probably glass.

Magnet: A small magnet is handy for detecting steel.

Onyx has parallel alternating bands of color, as white and brown or white and black.

Pewter feels slippery and shines when rubbed with lemon.

Ribs were added to sides of modern plastic thimbles to prevent rolling.

Silver: A bit of tarnish nearly always remains in the knurling of thimbles and can be detected by smell.

Tortoise shell smells like sea weed.

Vegetable ivory smells like burnt walnut shells.

Wax melted in the cap of a thimble may prevent fingernails from breaking.

INDEX OF
WELL-KNOWN THIMBLES

References to Book 1 are to a previous volume by the same author, "The Book of a Thousand Thimbles," 1970, Wallace-Homestead Book Co.